YOUR KNOWLEDGE HAS VALUE

Bibliographic information published by the German National Library:

The German National Library lists this publication in the National Bibliography; detailed bibliographic data are available on the Internet at http://dnb.dnb.de .

Imprint:

Copyright © 2018 GRIN Verlag
Print and binding: Books on Demand GmbH, Norderstedt Germany
ISBN: 9783668812581

This book at GRIN:

https://www.grin.com/document/443740

Ezekiel Oseni

Youth Unemployment. The Challenges of Skill Gap

GRIN Verlag

GRIN - Your knowledge has value

Since its foundation in 1998, GRIN has specialized in publishing academic texts by students, college teachers and other academics as e-book and printed book. The website www.grin.com is an ideal platform for presenting term papers, final papers, scientific essays, dissertations and specialist books.

Visit us on the internet:

http://www.grin.com/

http://www.facebook.com/grincom

http://www.twitter.com/grin_com

A

CONVOCATION LECTURE

TITLED

YOUTH UNEMPLOYMENT: THE CHALLENGES OF SKILL GAP

DELIVERED AT THE 2018 GRADUATION CEREMONY

OF

GATEWAY ICT POLYTECHNIC,
SAPAADE REMO,
OGUN STATE

NIGERIA

By

Dr. Ezekiel Oseni
Chief Risk Officer
Bank of Industry
23 Marina,
Lagos, Nigeria

SEPTEMBER 2018

Contents

Background 3

Introduction 3

Effects of youth unemployment on the Nigerian economy 6

Challenges of Skill Gap 8

Conclusion 13

References 17

Salutation

The Visitor, His Excellency Alh. Ibikunle Amosun, The Executive Governor, Ogun State
The Chairman and distinguished members of this Institution's Governing Council,
The Rector, Dr. Isaiah Kolawole Olayinka. Let me pause to congratulate you on your re-appointment after a successful and impactful first term as the Rector of this great institution of learning. You need not be reminded that the reward for hard work is more work. I wish you a more impactful second term.
The Registrar, Mrs. T. O. Raji
Other Principal Officers,
The Heads of Academic and Non-academic Departments,
The academic and non-academic staff members,
The students of this great institution,
Today's graduates and future leaders,
Gentlemen of the Press
Distinguished ladies and gentlemen.

Background

This lecture will be focusing on "Youth Unemployment: The Challenges of Skill Gap. In other words, I will be looking at the "mismatch between the demand for labour in the corporate worlds and the supply of labour by educational institutions".

I believe the topic at hand is timely, given the incessant rise in unemployment that has plagued Nigeria for years now—and which, as new graduates, some of you will likely face.

Once again, I congratulate the Rector on behalf of this institution for not only being sensitive to the challenges in the labour market but also for being responsive by trying to find solutions to the problems. This is the kind of responses needed to move the nation forward.

Introduction

One of the major challenges confronting Nigeria today is the high rate of unemployment among the youths. Every year, Nigerian higher institutions of learning turn out fresh graduates in their thousands while hundreds of those that studied abroad return to the country after the completion of their pogrammes to join their counterparts in search of jobs. The rate at which some of the educational institutions, especially private universities turn out graduates with first class and upper class grades are so alarming compared with a decade or two ago to the extent that one is tempted to ask whether the new graduates are more brilliant than their predecessors or is it a reflection of what many would like to refer to as declining quality of education? The irony is that many of these super grade graduates are not better off than their mates with lower grades in the labour market, in terms of quick access to employment or delivering on the jobs. They lack the skills required at the workplace in spite of their academic qualifications.

There are several reasons that have been adduced or deduced by scholars for the high unemployment rates in Nigeria. Some of the reasons have to do with harsh business environments and difficulties in doing business in Nigeria which have either restrained the growth capabilities of existing industries, forced some to liquidate or relocate from Nigeria and discouraged new ones from emerging (Imoisi, Amba and Okon, 2017; Ogunbanjo, et. al, 2017; Salami, 2013). The nation's real sector remains largely undeveloped thereby limiting available jobs. For instance, the development and job potentials of the primary agriculture and agro-processing sector, and its value chain lie in waste. Agriculture remains largely subsistent rather than commercial; its implements are crude rather than mechanized farming system. A substantial proportion of produce of the farms rot between the farms and the cities, a substantial portion of those not wasted are exported as raw materials for industries in advanced economies who either process them into finished goods or improved raw materials for our economy. The story of the solid mineral sector is not in any way different from the Agriculture sector.

Therefore, the Nigerian businesses have not been able to achieve the scale of development of global peers because of the challenges we face as a nation; such as infrastructural deficits (like power, transportation), macroeconomic instability, and socio-political issues, among others. Our businesses are therefore unable to grow to full capacity and create sufficient employment opportunities! Even the education sector is affected by these challenges that limit investment in the sector.

Other reasons for high rate of unemployment among the Nigerian youths which are very relevant to our subject of discussions have to do with the quality of the labour

4

seekers and the relevance of their education to the skills required in the work place (Longe, 2017; Chidiebere, Iloanya and Udunze, 2014; Uddin, Uddin and Osemengbe, 2013). The proponents of this second school of thought argue that though available job vacancies are few compared with the number of unemployed people out there, yet the skills required are absent as those in need of jobs lack the skill required by the employers of labour. Indeed, there is a disconnect between employers of labour and educational institutions. Employers complain that the curricula of higher institutions of learning have not evolved through the years with the changing business environment

Let me pause to note that unemployment is not a Nigeria problem. It is indeed a global problem. The major differences between nations are the unemployment rate and the intensity of the impact on the economy.

According to the World Employment and Social Outlook: Trends 2018, the global unemployment rate was put at 6.6%. The International Labour Organisation puts global unemployment in 2018 around 5.6%. That's equivalent to about 192 million people across the planet without jobs. In Sub-Sahara Africa, the unemployment rate is expected to rise to 7.2%. The report also noted that:

i)   More than one out of every three workers live in conditions of extreme poverty

ii)   Three out of every four worker is in vulnerable employment

iii) The global economy is not creating enough jobs

In Nigeria, according to the Nigerian Bureau of Statistics (2017), the general unemployment rates are 14.2% (Q4, 2016), 16.2% (Q2, 2017) and 18.8% (Q3, 2017). The number of people searching for jobs (unemployed and underemployed) increased from 31.3 Million (37.2%) in Q2, 2017 to 33.9 Million (40.0%) in Q3, 2017 Youth unemployment rate for Q3, 2017 was 33.1% for age 15 to 24 years and 20.2% for those between 25 and 34 years old. As of Q3, 2017, 67.3% of young people 15-24 years were either unemployed or underemployed (work for less than 20 hours a week, low skilled

5

jobs not commensurate with worker skills and qualifications). This was an increase from 64.6% of Q2, 2017. Similarly, the combined unemployment and underemployment rate for ages 25 to 34 years was 42.5% Q3, 2017 compared with 39.6% Q2, 2017. The combined unemployment and underemployment rate for all the youths (15-34 years) was 52.65% in Q3, 2017 compared to 45.65% Q3, 2016, 47.41% Q4, 2016 and 49.7% Q2, 2017. Think about that for a moment: Nigeria alone is responsible for about 8.3% of global unemployment. A single country, albeit an overpopulated one, accounting for almost 10% of global unemployment. And that country is ours. Worse still is the fact that our nation's youth unemployment is estimated at 30%, higher than the overall national unemployment rate of 18.8%.

Effects of youth unemployment on the Nigerian economy

The effects of youth unemployment are many, and their level of impact differ across nations. In Nigeria, the effects of youth unemployment include:

(i)   High rate of crimes

One of the attendant issues of high rate of unemployment is an exponential increase in the crime rates. Unemployed youths are more vulnerable to take to crimes than other categories of unemployed. There is a direct and significant relationship between unemployment and crime rates. Some of the crimes that are very attractive to unemployed youths include financial crimes, robbery, kidnapping, fraud and forgery, prostitution and terrorism.

i)   Brain Drain and Loss of Expertise.

Many unemployed youths who could not find jobs in Nigeria have found solace in other nations especially Europe and America. For instance, medical doctors, code writers, software engineers and a host of other professionals required to join us to develop our country have relocated abroad in search of greener pastures after years of unemployment or underemployment. We train for others to reap. One recent instance is the case of Nigerian trained Dr. Oluyinka Olutoye, a co-director of Texas Children's Foetal Center

6

who performed a surgical operation on a foetus that had a tumor, sutured her back in and delivered the baby through a Caesarean Section at full term. What he did was unprecedented in the medical history. He probably relocated abroad after his medical training because there was no vacancy in any of our well-equipped hospitals.

ii)   Slows down economic growth

Incomes empower the spending ability of the citizenry which in turn impacts on productivity and wellbeing of the economy. The higher the rate of unemployment, the more the people that are deprived of incomes that could have triggered economic growth. The government's ability to generate revenues through taxes and levies that could have been deployed for more economic growth is also denied by the unemployed individuals.

iii)   Inequality of income

The higher the unemployment rate, the wider the gap between the rich and the poor. The poor population is usually in the majority, and they are the first to be hit by the effects of unemployment. The gap between the extremely rich and poor is getting wider, almost eroding the middle-class that have a higher propensity to purchase and effectively contribute to the growth of the nation.

(ii)   Decrease in the nation's life expectancy ratio

It is expected that a nation with high unemployment rate and no welfare facilities for the unemployed would likely record higher mortality rates resulting from malnutrition, lack of timely and proper medicare and depression.

(iii)   Increase in birth rate.

Unemployed people who stay at home most of the days are likely to engage in sexual activities to while away time and dissipate their unused energy with no intention to procreate but which often end in procreation. The poor and unemployed tend to produce more children than the rich because they have more idle time to themselves.

As a father, this issue of unemployment, especially among the youths, is dear to my heart. I cannot but agree with studies that describe youth unemployment as weapons of destruction or as potentially dangerous (Oyelola, et. al. 2014; Adesina, 2013; Okafor, 2011). As Nigerians, it is an issue we must all address collectively and urgently.

I am a teacher and a researcher, but I have chosen not to dwell too much on the factors I earlier mentioned and along with other ones that conspired to push up Nigeria's unemployment rate. There are tonnes of research work on that already.

Rather, I have chosen for the purpose of this occasion to focus on what is of most concern to the young men and women for whom we are all gathered here today, and it is this: how does this state of affairs affect you and how should we all react to the challenges of skill gap in addressing unemployment?

Let me start with how it affects you. Well, it affects you in many important ways.

Challenges of Skill Gap

A study of the big impact of soft skills in today's workplace by Binsaeed, Unnisa and Rizvi (2017) revealed that in spite of the many job opportunities from globalization, privatization and technology advancement, many youths still find it very difficult to get jobs. In other words, despite high unemployment rates in many countries, employers struggle to find adequately qualified personnel to fill the vacant positions.

While graduates place emphasis on academic qualifications, the employers are looking for skilled candidates. The market is in high need of employees that possess both hard and soft skills in good proportions. One of the major causes of unemployment is the wide gap between skill required in the workplace and skill possessed by the job seekers. A survey of the private sector by Barthel, et. al. (2016) shows that the prevalence of skills gaps in many developing and emerging countries is attributable to the inability of the nations' public education systems to equip people with the right skills.

Research studies have shown that most employers in the corporate world in Nigeria do not believe that graduates are adequately trained or prepared for the job market (Ayonmike and Okeke, 2016; Muo, 2016; Okuntade, 2015; Sodipo, 2014). Employers are aware that there are many unemployed people in the country, but they do not believe the required skills are there. They believe there is a mismatch between the theory-based skills graduates have acquired from academic institutions and the actual practical skills they need to work. Obadic (2006) believes that possession of the right skills by job seekers would drastically reduce unemployment rates.

About 40% of employers have difficulty finding candidates with the right skills. It is also becoming more common to find graduates in jobs that do not match their hard and soft skill requirements. About 30% of graduates are in jobs that do not even require a higher learning degree - a waste of their talents and a source of immense personal frustration.

The reality of today is that manpower requirements in the work place are fast changing (Ukpong, 2017; Wajiga and Ndaghu, 2017). They change with new products, new processes, new technologies, new markets and demographic shifts. But the educational curriculum in many of our higher institutions of learning remain mostly unchanged. Many of our institutions continue to produce new graduates that are possibly fit for the needs of decades ago, hardly for the present and certainly not for the future needs of the employers and the society. Almost every corporate job requires skill which Sharma and Sethi (2015) defined as the set of competencies essential to carry out the required tasks in the most efficient way while maintaining the agreed set of quality standards. They are two sets of skills: Hard and soft. Hard skills refer to specific and technical abilities to execute a particular job (Cimatti, 2016; Sharma and Sethi, 2015). The ability of a software engineer to write codes is the hard skill and the ability of an accountant to prepare the books in accordance with statutory and regulatory requirements is the hard skill. According to Arat (2014), hard skill is a product of academic education and practical experience. The hard skills required in the 1990s and 2000s are certainly inadequate for today's job requirements. The changing business needs cut across every profession, every facet of life.

Let me also talk about the soft skill. According to Cimatti (2016), the term soft skills can be described as all competences that are not directly connected to a specific task but necessary in any position as they mainly refer to the relationship with other people in the organization. These are the personal attributes of the individuals. Schulz (2008) described it as education beyond academic knowledge. While an employee needs hard skills at work, soft skills are required everywhere. Many employers prefer it to hard skill. An employee with excellent soft skill and average hard skill is more preferable to the one with excellent hard skill and poor soft skill. Every year, more and more graduates struggle with the very soft skills that employers value and prioritize: critical thinking, problem-solving, leadership, ownership, teamwork, communication, and independent decision making.

Skills gap is a term usually used to describe the difference between the skills needed for a job and those possessed by a worker. It represent a major constraint to the nation's economic development. It is the gap between theoretical knowledge and practical knowledge (Scully, 2011). The challenges of skill gaps to a nation that is plagued a by high level of youth unemployment can be enormous and the effects very devastating.

There are three levels to the challenges and effects of skill gaps:

i)   For the individual, skill gaps limit employability and deprive an individual of the opportunity to improve his or her living conditions.

ii)   At the company level, skill gaps limit productivity, which can lead to higher costs and lower quality, and reduce the company's growth prospects. Retraining employees to fit into the business skill requirements is at huge costs. The financial costs and time involved to bring the employee to the required standards can be enormous while competitors could take advantage of those avoidable distractions to take more of the market share for themselves.

iii)   At the country level, skill gaps limit the nation's competitiveness and reduce economic and social development potentials. Studies have revealed that a direct relationship exists between unemployment and national output, however, it is negative. The Okun's law established that because output is directly and proportionately related to quantity of labour in production process that is labour intensive, the relationship between unemployment and output is therefore inverse (Okun, 1962). The nation's economic growth and development are further worsened where both inflation and unemployment rates are very high.

With all these challenges of securing jobs in a nation like ours, is there hope for the fresh graduates and unemployed youths? Yes, there is. Job opportunities abound. As a fresh graduate, you may want to throw up your hands and say, "Why did I even bother studying so hard?" Don't be so quick to quit !!!. I assure you, however, that all of these obstacles are actually areas of opportunity for all you graduates sitting here today.

Let's look at these jobs that don't require degrees and diplomas. Not all of them are run-of-the-mill, go-nowhere, low-level positions. Just last month, it was well publicized that an increasing number of companies no longer insist that candidates have a traditional university degree—industry leaders like Google, Amazon, Ernst & Young, even Apple. These companies emphasize hard skills (knowledge skills) and soft skills over education for their high-paying "new collar jobs," that is, jobs for which you can acquire skills through vocational training, apprenticeships, or certificate programmes. They are looking for you.

If as a graduate of Computer science, you are able to write codes to solve problems or resolve some network or hardware issues, they are looking for you. If as a graduate of Engineering you are able to make designs or resolve engineering related problems, as a graduate of Accounting, Marketing, Mass Communication you are able to solve problems in the workplace, they are looking for you. The world is changing. Nobody will ask you anymore to define computer, accounting or marketing at interviews. Employers are looking for who can deliver, who possess knowledge and soft skills and not who can memorize books.

This brings me to another matter that is close to my heart.

There is a growing sector that is providing more professional opportunities for today's youths, a sector that unemployment statistics overlook. I speak of Nigeria's creative industries. These industries are focused on two goals: the creation and exploration of knowledge and information, and entrepreneurship. Some of you have studied Computer Science, Accountancy, Mass Communication, but you are also Graphic Designers,

11

Marketing Consultants, Writers, Film Producers, Artists, Fashion Designers, Stylists, and Entertainers.

The "new age" jobs of today's creative industries may not be captured in the broad definition of the employed, but they are vital to the economy nevertheless. As entrepreneurs, you have to be highly creative, inventive, and innovative. As entrepreneurs, you have to possess the innate ability to sense opportunity, act on it, and deliver something new to the world. As entrepreneurs, you leverage on your talents, create opportunities for yourself, and will one day be responsible for employing a vast number of other youths. You don't have to fall into the category of those who hold jobs that do not match their skills—instead, create opportunities that do.

Now, because candidates today are increasingly being considered based on their knowledge and skills and not necessarily on how the knowledge and skills were acquired, some would argue that you don't need a higher learning education to become an entrepreneur or secure gainful employment. I would, however, counter that the value of a solid education is indisputable, so much so that it has been classified as a human right in most societies! A higher learning degree provides a rigorous foundation that will serve you well in your career and is indeed a great achievement. You just have to leverage that achievement. Armed with the right skills that you have acquired during your higher education, you are better prepared for active citizenship. You have a better chance of finding and keeping a good job. You are better equipped to set up your own business—and, in turn, create jobs for others.

Therefore, you can leverage on the diplomas you have earned today to build a fulfilling career and, through your labour help grow the economy and move the country forward, so that others after you can do the same. But how do you accomplish this when the market continues to believe that most graduates are ill-prepared for the workplace? Well, you cannot on your own. We must all work together in our various complementary capacities to change the narrative. So while the government continues making efforts toward developing an enabling environment for institutions and citizens alike, we all have active parts to play in actuating a positive and desired turnaround.

Conclusion

i) To my venerable colleagues in academia for I have been a member of the academic community for the past 28 years now. Though I am no longer in full time academics, I still teach in universities (bringing practice to the classroom and blending theories with practice) and I publish academic papers regularly alongside my regular job) and to the various policymakers in this enterprise. We need to forge stronger links between the worlds of classroom education and practice. Educational institutions must place greater emphasis on complementing theoretical knowledge with both practical knowledge (knowledge skills) and soft skills development, which are important to employers if they will continue to occupy their esteemed position in the society. The educational curricula and training programmes should be regularly reviewed within a space of not more than two years, to enable them capture the changing needs of the labour market and the society. In your dissipation of knowledge, bring practice to the classroom. Not all resources in the academics possess the practical experience. So the educational institutions may need to accommodate professionals in practice to share the hard skills (knowledge skill) and the soft skills in addition to the conventional theoretical education the students are being exposed to. This way, you will ensure that the specialty areas you offer students are based on the current and future skill needs of the labour market.

ii) To the esteemed corporate organisations represented here: You must actively seek to collaborate with educational institutions. You must begin to view them, not just as a repository of knowledge, but also as a route to the solutions you seek for the challenges your industries face. There should be a handshake between practice and classrooms. Feedbacks from employers of labour would help the educational institutes update their curricula in line with the future needs of the labour market. The corporate organizations should take up this responsibility through symposia, press releases and other collaborations to provide feedbacks to the institutions.

iii) To our remarkable youths, all of you who graduate today as well as others present: The job of closing the skill gaps between educational institutions and the industry does not reside only with government, institutions, and industries. You are the ones who stand to be most directly affected by the mismatch. You, therefore, have a critical part to play.

The reality is that some of you may face difficulties as you seek employment because you have spent most of your education focusing on getting good grades and have to this point paid little attention to improving your soft skills.

Graduation from a college or university does not guarantee employment, as students often have not acquired the skills that employers demand. To succeed in the labour market, people need a broad range of both hard skills, such as knowledge of accounting practices or the ability to operate machinery – and soft skills, such as creativity, leadership, flexibility, work ethics, interpersonal, problem solving and communication skills.

But I say to all of you here: Do not be afraid. Do not give up on the opportunities that the Nigerian environment offers. You can change the perception that employers have of graduates and you can forge your own path.

First, you must look inward, reflect, and critically assess your skills—your leadership, analytical, communication, and critical reasoning skills—and be honest with yourself about your shortcomings. Then you must work hard to eliminate those shortcomings. Remember: no one was born with their abilities—everyone develops them. I firmly believe that if each of you puts your mind to it, you can all transform whatever weaknesses you have into strengths, especially with the resources at your fingertips

As today's youths, you are more fortunate than any who have come before you. You have two essential advantages that previous generations did not have: open and available knowledge and technology. Use these extraordinary resources to develop your skills and yourselves first. (You can do Instagram,

Snapchat, and selfies later. Those applications are useful, by the way, when you use them to improve your professional—and not just social—standing, so take advantage of them to do just that.)

Remember, the right skills open doors to new possibilities. With the right skills in the workforce, you can make businesses more competitive and organizations more effective. You can grow our economy faster, and by doing so, you can create more jobs and better jobs.

The road that lies ahead won't be easy. There will be obstacles and missed exits, potholes and roadblocks. There will be times when some of you will feel like giving up. Dear graduates, this graduation has already shown me that you are capable of accomplishing great goals when you commit yourselves to them.

So as you step into the world, don't see challenges—see opportunities. Take control of your destiny. You, as they say, hold the keys to the kingdom. You have what you need within yourselves to secure your future and, therefore, Nigeria's future. So go into that outside world better than you exit this institution. I charge you to enter the world with confidence. Enter with hope and determination. Enter with grace. Enter with fortitude. Enter with the mind that you will not be a liability, but an asset, that you will make positive impacts on yourself, your family, our dear nation and the world at large. Dear graduates, the future belongs to you, that future begins now and here, take hold of it and don't mess it up. Remember, time flies !!!

iv) Once again, I congratulate this year's class of graduates and I congratulate all the builders of these great destinies waiting to make the world a better place to live. Behind each of these wonderful graduates here today is a story of family and friends; of parents who nourished and sacrificed; who hovered and let go; of grandparents, uncles and aunts who supported and sustained them; of brothers, sisters, cousins, and friends, who stood by them and with them; of spouses and loved ones who strengthened and inspired them. Here are the results of your efforts and sacrifices.

Congratulations!!!

Thank you all for your time.

References

Adesina, O. S. (2013). Unemployment and Security Challenges in Nigeria. *International Journal of Humanities and Social Science Vol. 3 (7): 146 – 156*
Arat, M. (2014). Acquiring soft skills at university. *Journal of Educational and Instructional Studies, Vol. 4(3)*: 46 – 51
Ayonmike, C. S. and Okeke, B. C. (2016). Bridging the skills gap and tackling unemployment of vocational graduates through partnerships in Nigeria. *Journal of Technical Education and Training, Vol. 8(2)*: 1 - 11
Barthel, F. et. al. (2016). Bridging the skills gaps in developing countries: A practical guide for private-sector companies. https://www.bcg.com/publications/2016/bridging-the-skills-gap-in-developing-countries.aspx
Binsaeed, R. H., Unnisa, S. T. and Rizvi, L. J. (2017). The big impact of soft skills in today's workplace. *International Journal of Economics, Commerce and Management, Vol V(1)*: 456 – 463
Cimatti, B. (2016). Definition, development. Assessment of soft skills and their role for the quality of organizations and enterprises. *International Journal for Quality Research, Vol. 10(1)*: 97 – 130
Imoisi, A. I., Amba. E. A. and Okon I. M. (2017). Unemployment rate and economic growth in Nigeria: An empirical analysis (1980-2016). *International Journal of Development Sustainability, Vol. 6(7)*: 369 – 384
Longe, O. (2017). Graduate unemployment in Nigeria: Causes, consequences and remediable approaches. *American International Journal of Contemporary Research, Vol. 7 (4)*: 63 – 73
Muo, I. K. (2016). Skill mismatch and employability in Nigeria: A review of literature. *Journal of Advances in Humanities, Vol. 4 (5)*: 575 – 579
Nigerian Bureau of Statistics (2017). http://nigerianstat.gov.ng/
Obadic, A. (2006).Theoretical and empirical framework of measuring mismatch on a labour market. *Proceedings of Rijeka Faculty of Economics: Journal of Economics and Business (zbornik@efri.hr); Vol.24 (1)*: 55-80.
Ogunbanjo, O. A. et. al. (2017). Causes and effects of graduate unemployment on the Nigerian economy (the case study of Lagos State). *Asian Research Journal of Arts and Social Sciences, Vol. 2(1)*: 1 – 10
Okafor, E. (2011). Youth unemployment and implications for stability of democracy in Nigeria. *Journal of Sustainable Development in Africa, Vol. 13 (1)*: 358 -373
Okun, A. M. (1962). Potential GNP: Its measurement and significance. *American Statistical Association, Proceedings of the Business and Economics Statistics Section*: 98 -104
Okuntade, T. F. (2015). Shortage of skills workers in the Nigerian construction industry: A paradigm of a failed government policy.
Oyelola, O. T. et. al. (2014). Entrepreneurship education: Solution to youth unemployment in Nigeria. *Journal of Poverty, Investment and Development, Vol. 5*: 149 – 157

Salami, C. G. E. (2013). Youth unemployment in Nigeria: A time for creative intervention. *International Journal of Business and Marketing Management, Vol. 1(2)*: 18 – 26

Schulz, B. (2008). The importance of soft skills: Education beyond academic knowledge. *Journal of Language and Communication*: 146 – 154

Scully, N. J. (2011). The theory-practice gap and skill acquisition: An issue for nursing education. *The Australian Journal of Nursing Practice*, Vol. 18 (2): 93–98

Sharma, E. and Sethi, S. (2015). Skill development: Opportunities and challenges in India. *Gian Jyoti E-Journal, Vol. 5(1)*: 45 -55

Sodipo, O. O. (2014). Employability of tertiary education graduates in Nigeria: Closing the skills-Gap' *Global Journal of Human Resource Management, Vol. 2(3)*: 28 -36

The International Labour Organisation (2018). https://www.ilo.org/global/lang--en/index.htm

Uddin, P.S.O. and Uddin, O. O. Causes, effects and solutions to youth unemployment problems in Nigeria. *Journal of Emerging Trends in Economics and Management Sciences (JETEMS), Vol. 4(4)*: 397 – 402

Ukpong, E. A. (2017). Developing a national manpower planning policy for Nigeria: The shifts and new fundamentals. *Journal of Social Science for Policy Implications, Vol. 5 (2)*: 21 -33

Wajiga, H. and Ndaghu, J. T. (2017). Significance of manpower planning for effective utilization of human resources in an organization: A conceptual approach. *International Journal of Business and Management Invention, Vol. 6(8)*: 16 – 22.

World Employment and Social Outlook: Trends 2018. http://www.ilo.org/global/research/global-reports/weso/2018/WCMS_615594/lang--en/index.htm